*Tequila* **Mockingbird**

"The body is eighty-two percent broth."

# Tequila Mockingbird

A Book of Animal Cartoons

by Leo Cullum

Harry N. Abrams, Inc., Publishers

Editor: Christopher Sweet
Editorial Assistant: Sigi Nacson
Series Designer: Robert McKee
Designer: Miko McGinty and Maki Takenouchi
Production Manager: Maria Pia Gramaglia

Library of Congress Cataloging-in-Publication Data

Cullum, Leo.
   Tequila mockingbird : a book of animal cartoons / by Leo
Cullum.
      p. cm.
   ISBN 0-8109-4847-8 (hardcover)
   1. Animals—Caricatures and cartoons. 2. American wit
and humor,
Pictorial. I. Title.

NC1429.C84A4 2004
741.5'973—dc22
                              2003022523

Published in 2004 by Harry N. Abrams, Incorporated, New York.

Printed and bound in China.

10 9 8 7 6 5 4 3 2 1

Harry N. Abrams, Inc.
100 Fifth Avenue
New York, N.Y. 10011
www.abramsbooks.com

*"I love the convenience, but the roaming charges are killing me."*

*For my parents*

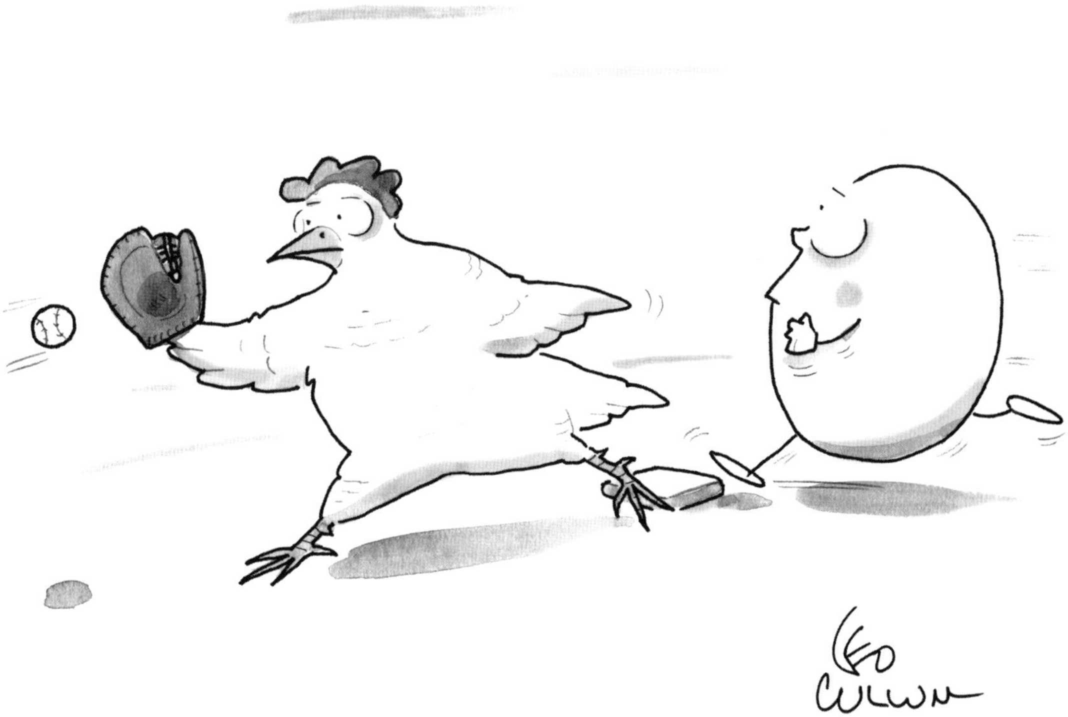
LEO CULLUM

*"Be careful. Your father went on-line and I haven't seen him since."*

# Introduction

Eons ago, a creature crawled out of the primordial ooze, walked upright, and then began crawling in the desert in search of water. That's the basic history of the earth, life, and the cartoon.

Today we share over ninety-nine percent of our DNA with the chimpanzees, and I say that's way too much. It's embarrassing for everyone concerned, but it does serve to emphasize our kinship with other living creatures, and we should learn to appreciate it. I appreciate it by trying to make people laugh and scoring a few bucks along the way.

My parents named me Leo, which in Latin means lion, but in English usually means grocer or accountant. Despite my high school struggles I prefer the Latin. From an early age I was fascinated with animals, particularly those at the Bronx Zoo. Why, I wondered, would they choose to live in the Bronx when the wilds of New Jersey were only a few miles away? Obviously, I didn't understand the function of the zoo. I still don't. Now, I'm told they're wonderful places, though I don't see any animals trying to break in.

For a cartoonist, animals definitely bring something to the drawing board, but, like some sitcom stars, they are not that funny without writers! (I do hear, however, that Henny Youngman's parrot can still get laughs.)

Animals are masters of metaphor: wise owls and birdbrained birds, laughing hyenas and crocodiles shedding tears, scared rabbits and lionhearted lions, busy beavers and slothful sloths. Does a horse have sense? Is a pig pigheaded? This is the arena of the cartoonist—to take an animal's personal cliché and blow it out of all reasonable proportion.

The chicken crossing the road may be second only to the desert island castaway in the number of cartoon appearances it can claim. Elephants, we know, never forget. But, more important, do they ever forgive? Fish, cows, birds, snakes . . . caught by the cartoonist's pen are all just deer in the headlights.

I feel it's my duty to do for some deserving animal what Walt Disney did for Mickey Mouse, and if in the process an enormous global entertainment behemoth is created, so be it. The proceeds will be shared equally among all the birds of the air and beasts of the field and any others who fill out the required paperwork. I happen to know that Mickey is still waiting for his first royalty cheese.

In the meantime, though I've stopped visiting zoos (actually no one has invited me), I continue to enjoy the company of the menagerie in my head—a peaceable kingdom where the lion can lie down with the lamb and laugh at its jokes, and the lamb hopes the lion keeps laughing. Wouldn't it be wonderful if the whole world kept laughing . . . and there were world peace . . . and this book sold a million copies. All we can do is pray.

*—Leo Cullum, 2003*

"I try not to be judgmental, but I see everything in black and white."

"He's o.k., but I can't give him a ringing endorsement."

"*That one, I think, is a liver spot.*"

*"We do a service to humanity by culling out the weak, the sick, and the surfers."*

*"Something in a pig's eye."*

*"Apparently you're a bi-polar bear."*

"I thought he was just huffing and puffing but he really was foreclosing."

"I understand they're not as likely to talk if you have two of them together."

"He does have a dark side, but it's mostly his back and thighs."

"It's like a business. Concentrate on the bottom lion."

*"Could you be more specific than 'woodland creature'?"*

"He was talking apples and I was talking oranges. No one said a thing about bananas!"

"I've taken a government handout not to grow any wool."

"*This part is easy. The tough part is instilling brand loyalty.*"

"It's going to be a long, cold winter. That's his third bowl of nuts."

*"We could reshape your nose with conventional surgery,
but I'm going to suggest something radical."*

"It's a fabulous deal. You'll make peanuts."

"You're kidding. I thought it was Friday."

"*When I first saw your mother, she was bathed in moonlight.*"

"'Extra goat cheese'? Like I don't have enough to do."

"*Quoth.*"

"How she's able to manage a career and still juggle her family, I'll never know."

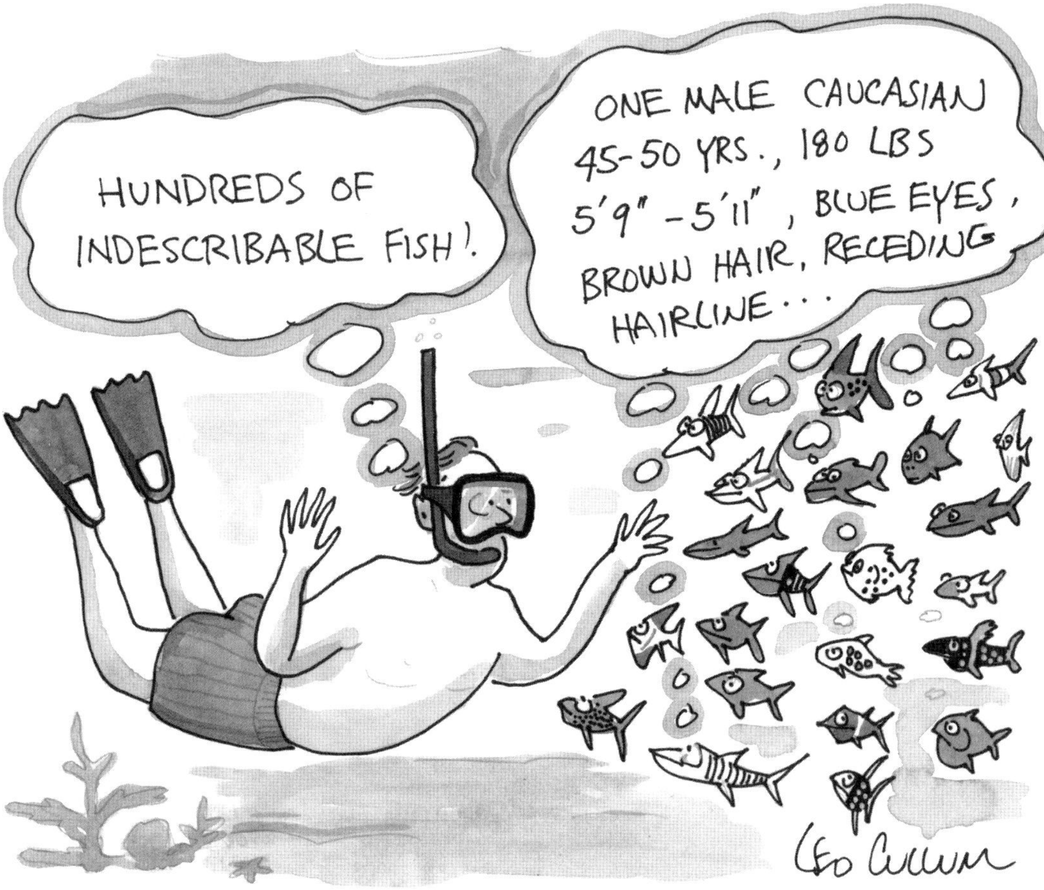
HUNDREDS OF INDESCRIBABLE FISH!
ONE MALE CAUCASIAN 45-50 YRS., 180 LBS 5'9" - 5'11", BLUE EYES, BROWN HAIR, RECEDING HAIRLINE...
LEO CULLUM

"*Your skin. Genuine leather.*"

"We're losing habitat, but we're extremely adaptable."

"He honks for peace but, of course, he honks for everything."

"*That's the catnip channel. We had to take it to get the cheese channel.*"

"*Two roads diverged in a wood and he tried to cross both of them.*"

"I have to ask . . . do you have any addictions?"

"Am I still your main squeeze?"

*"Another round?"*

"The cheese balls—can I get that as an entrée?"

"I got over DDT, and I'll get over you!"

*"In my practice, I prefer to treat the whole hog."*

"This is the beak I was born with and it's the beak I'll die with."

"You wouldn't understand . . . It's a poultry thing."

*"Have you ever heard anyone yell 'EEEK! A Psychiatrist!'?"*

"Barry made the wine. I made the cheese."

"Explain something to me. Are 'boned' and 'deboned' the same thing?"

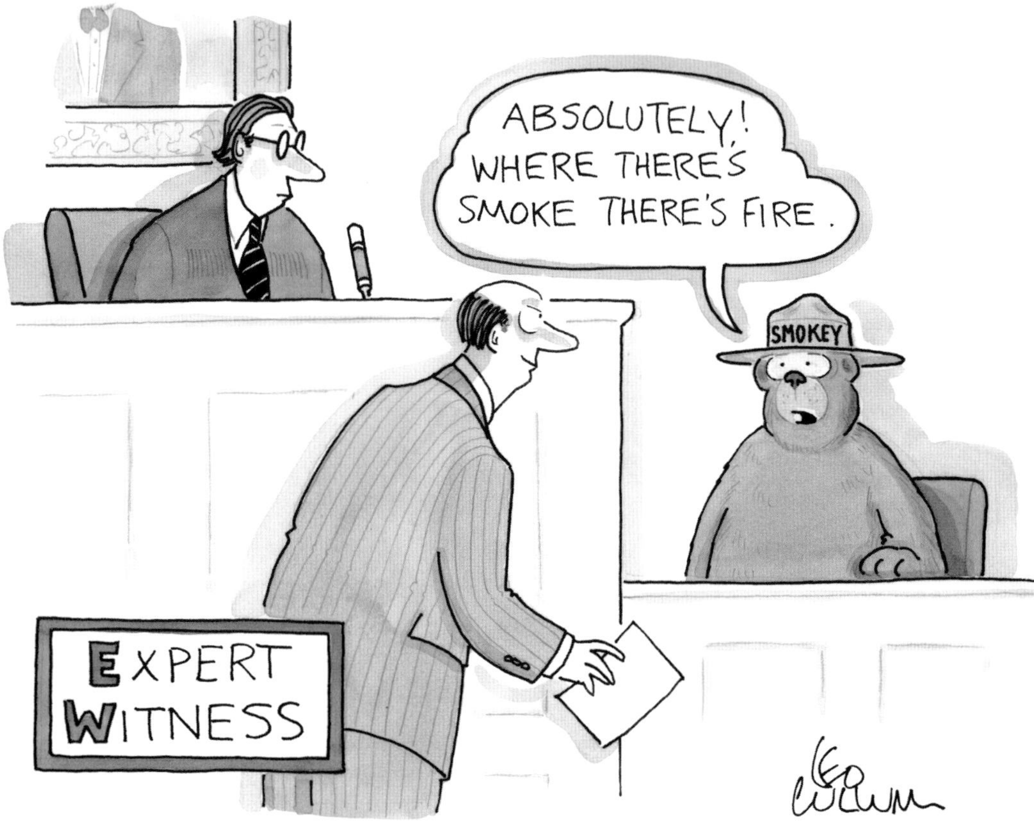
ABSOLUTELY! WHERE THERE'S SMOKE THERE'S FIRE.
SMOKEY
EXPERT WITNESS

"I've never written anything, but I think I have a good ear for dialogue."

*"Dear, I'd like you to meet the Holsteins."*

"Gimme a break. Being driven out of Ireland
was the best thing that ever happened to you."

"He damaged a nerve when he pulled the thorn out.
I'd have had a surefire malpractice suit if I hadn't eaten him."

"You're making more at this firm than anyone else whose brain is the size of a walnut."

*"You rang?"*

"He's a porcupine, and he's prickly. I accept that."

"You never tell me you're 'hog wild' about me anymore."

*"I'll be late, dear. My leg is in a trap."*

*"No one will ever take you seriously with those tassels."*

*"They tell me I have a firm consistency and a mild flavor. How about you?"*

"I do want to talk about your feelings but first let's talk about cheese."

"*You need a chicken–liver transplant.*"

"No, no, no! Serpentine, serpentine!!"

"*I'm not sure what I am, but I believe I'm a product of Norway.*"

*"Counting the space behind the pantry shelves, it's eleven square feet."*

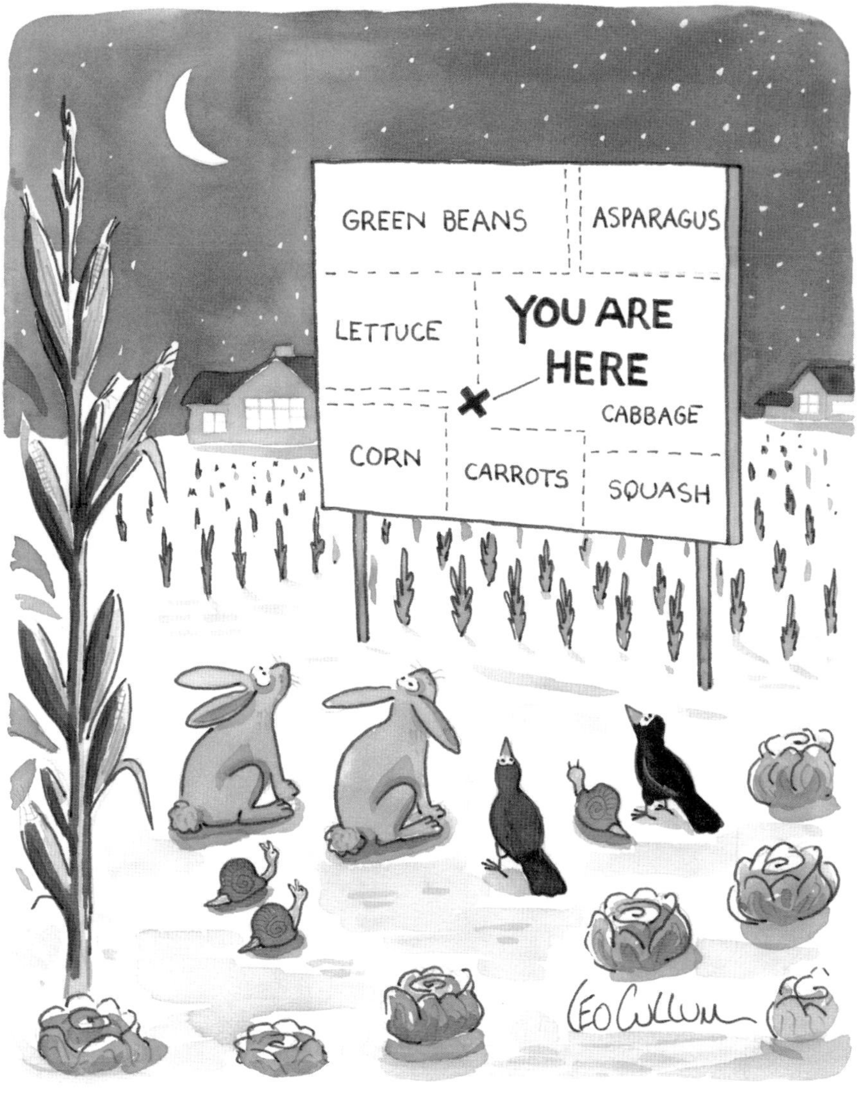
GREEN BEANS
ASPARAGUS
LETTUCE
YOU ARE HERE
CABBAGE
CORN
CARROTS
SQUASH
LEO CULLUM

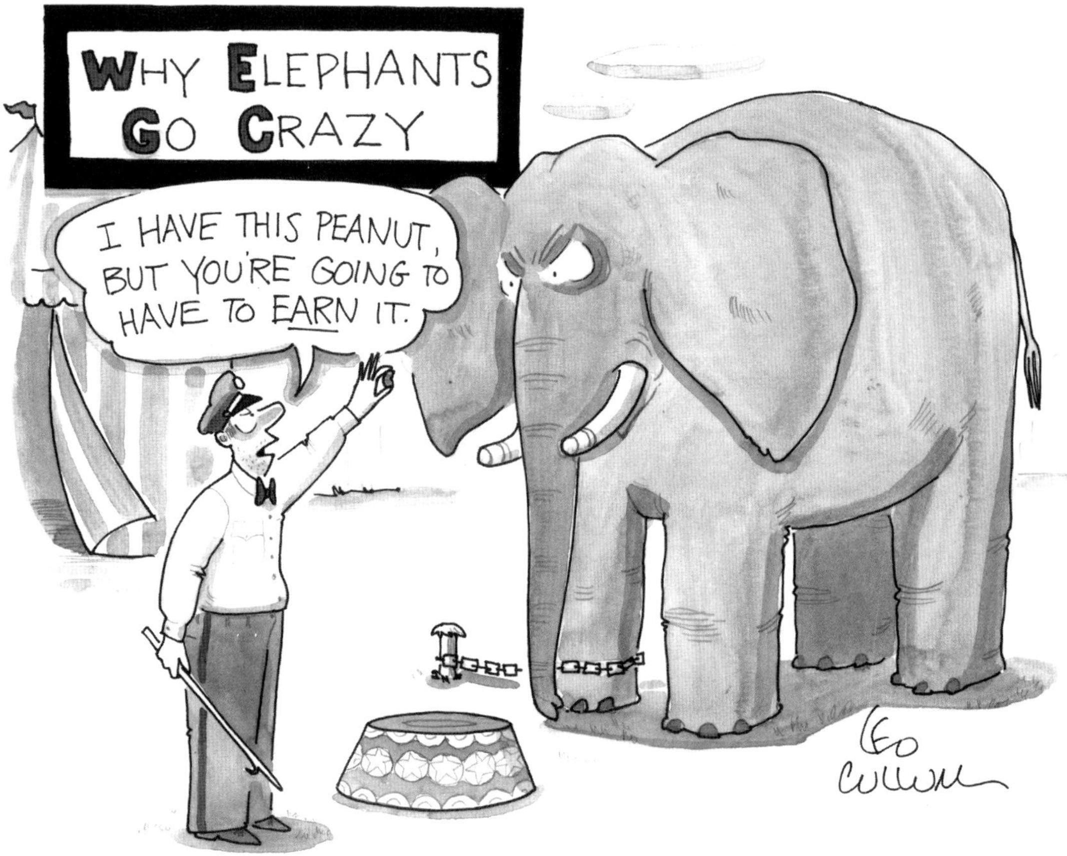
WHY ELEPHANTS GO CRAZY
I HAVE THIS PEANUT, BUT YOU'RE GOING TO HAVE TO EARN IT.
LEO CULLUM

*"The apple in his mouth . . . pippin, fuji, or granny smith?"*

*"You've had enough 'monkey see,' Edwards. We want some 'monkey do.'"*

*"It's early, so I'll just have the worm."*

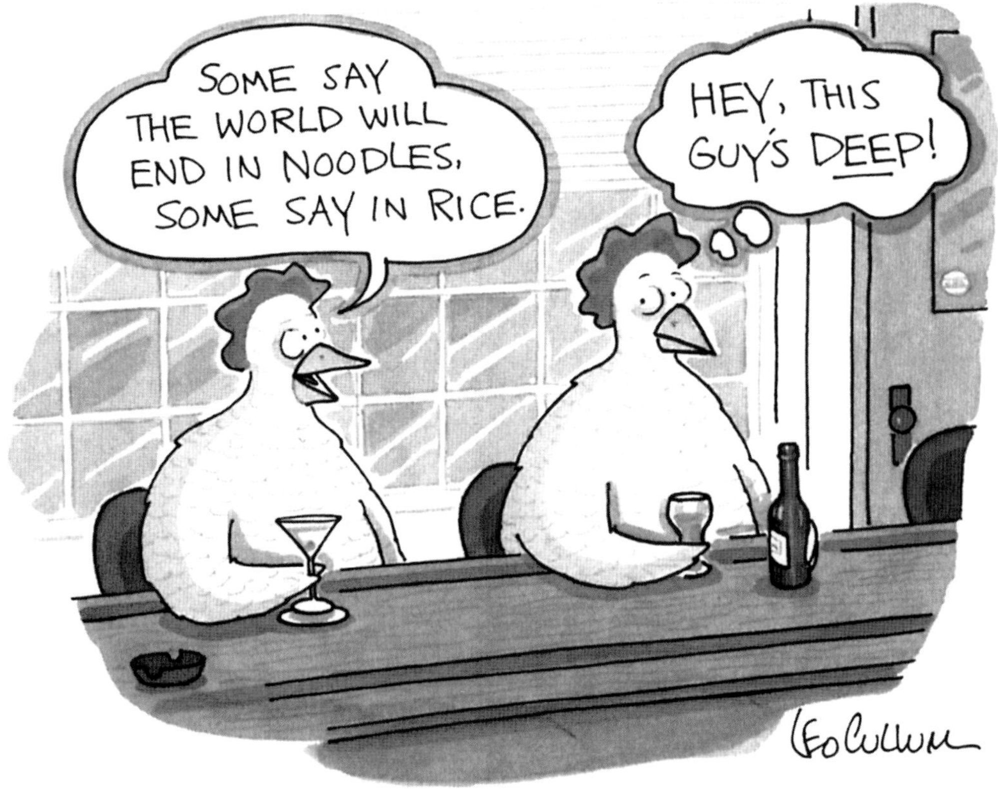
SOME SAY THE WORLD WILL END IN NOODLES, SOME SAY IN RICE.
HEY, THIS GUY'S DEEP!
LEO CULLUM

"He looks a little unusual, but he has a wonderful herd instinct."

"*Our products are cheesy and I'm most proud of that.*"

"You've got a piece of eco-tourist or something stuck between your teeth."

"Oh my God! I just stepped on something squishy."

"Let's turn up the heat very gradually on this guy."

"*Well, do we go out or stay home and open a can of worms?*"

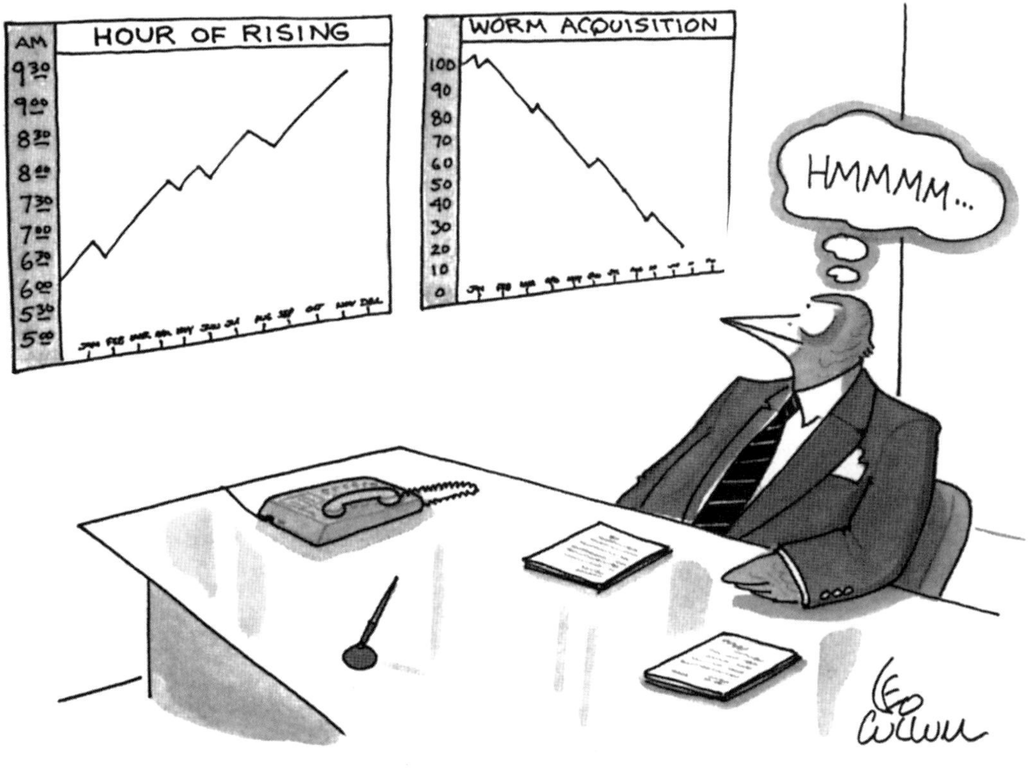
HOUR OF RISING
AM
9 30
9 00
8 30
8 00
7 30
7 00
6 30
6 00
5 30
5 00
WORM ACQUISITION
100
90
80
70
60
50
40
30
20
10
0
HMMMM...

*It's thornlike in appearance, but I need to order a battery of tests."*

"I may be a sardine, Ted, but I still need space."

"I love the way you use your bulk."

"Hey, I *built the nest*. You *feather it*."

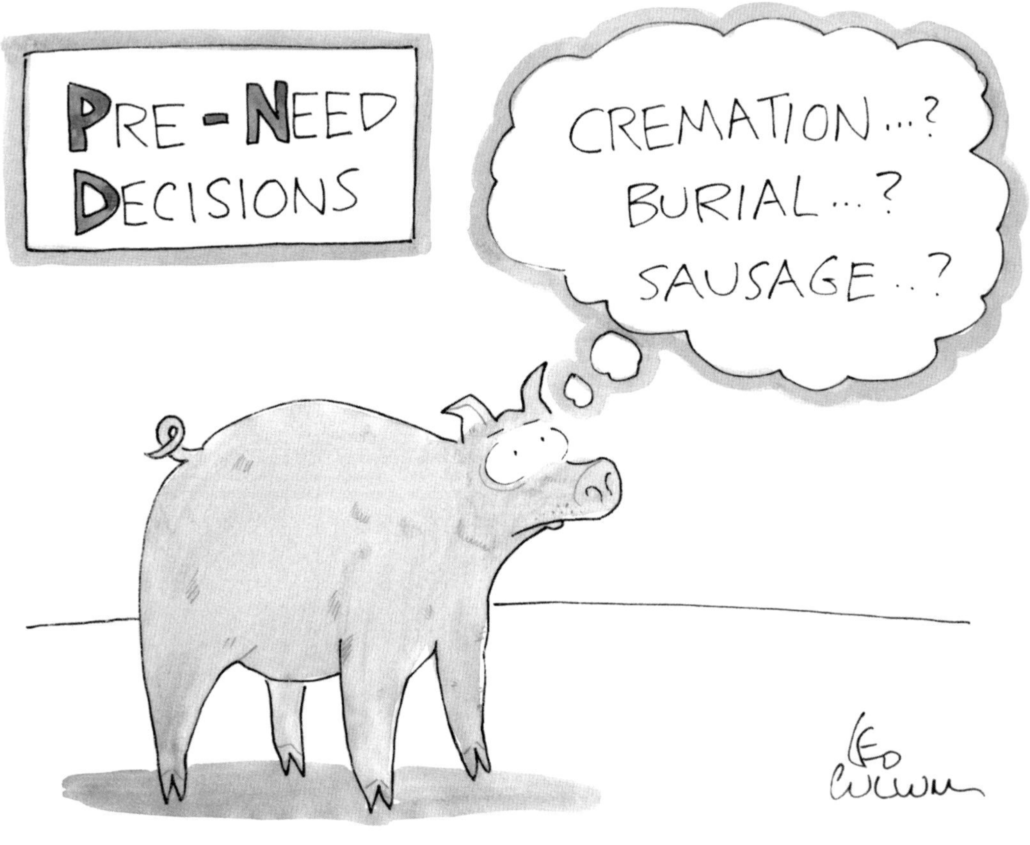
PRE-NEED DECISIONS
CREMATION...?
BURIAL...?
SAUSAGE..?

"The pectoral fins help with directional control. The rest is just decorative."

"It's all very 'hush-hush' but there have been startling advances in Aquaculture."

*"You know you have my support on pork and beans,
but where do you stand on chicken and dumplings?"*

*"You walk like a duck and you quack like a duck, Wilson, and I find it very patronizing."*

"If I ever meet an ostrich I'm going to buy it a drink."

"Have you ever wondered why we're carbo-loading when we don't run any marathons?"

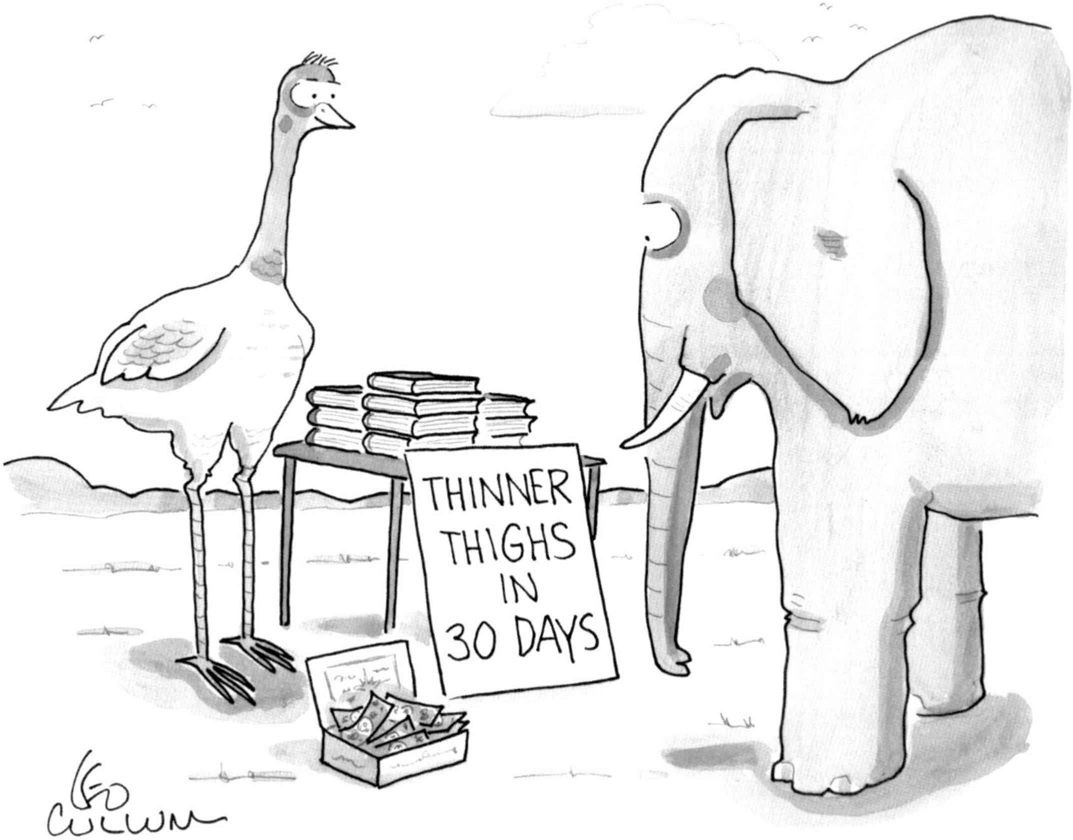
THINNER
THIGHS
IN
30 DAYS

"I don't have any money. I'm a mullet."

"Hi, honey. I think I'm home."

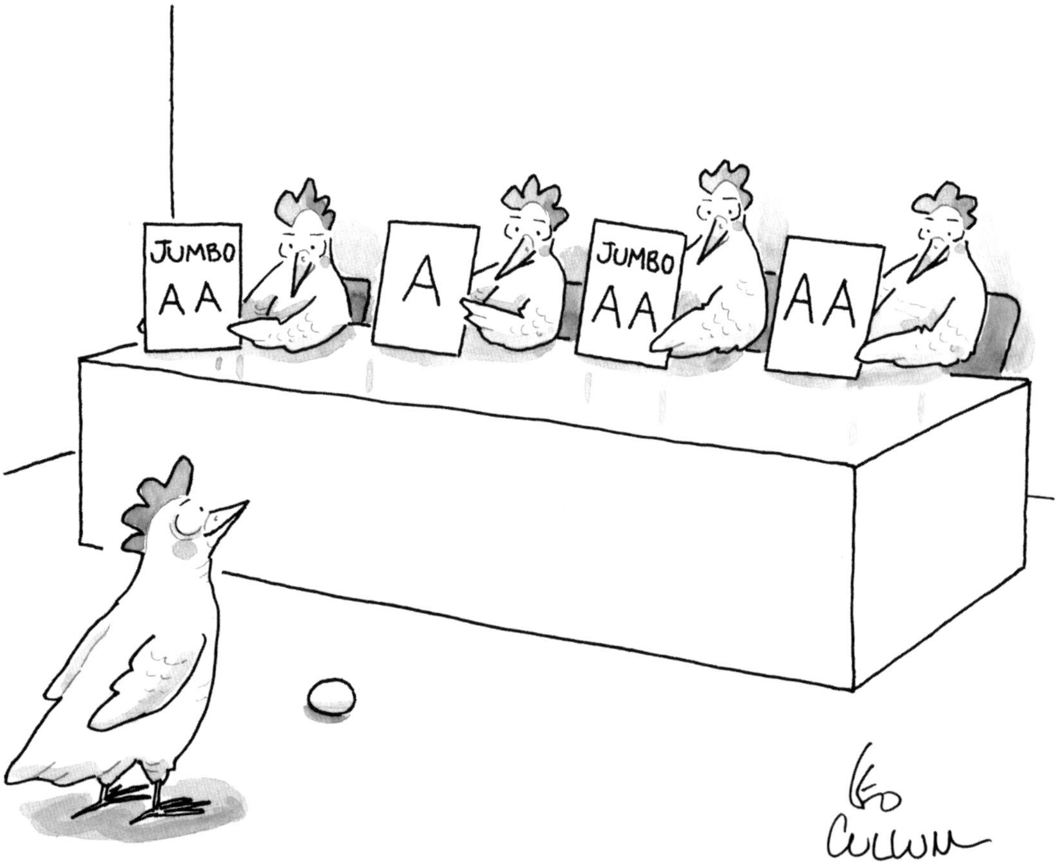
JUMBO AA
A
JUMBO AA
AA

"*That's not* my *political opinion. That's just stuff I hear on the radio.*"

"... and, what might 'the road' represent?"

"*Fortunately, the law of the jungle doesn't require lawyers of the jungle.*"

"*The ringing in your ears—I think I can help.*"

*"The fact is, Inez, I miss your nitpicking."*

"A cluck cluck here and a cluck cluck there,' . . . is that all I meant to you?"

*"We usually have a light breakfast, then a feeding frenzy in the early afternoon, and that's it for the day."*

"There goes our attorney, headed for Florida."

"Some will love you, son, and some will hate you.
It's always been that way with anchovies."

*"If we give you an office with a window, how do we know you won't fly away?"*

*"Try to think outside of the bowl."*

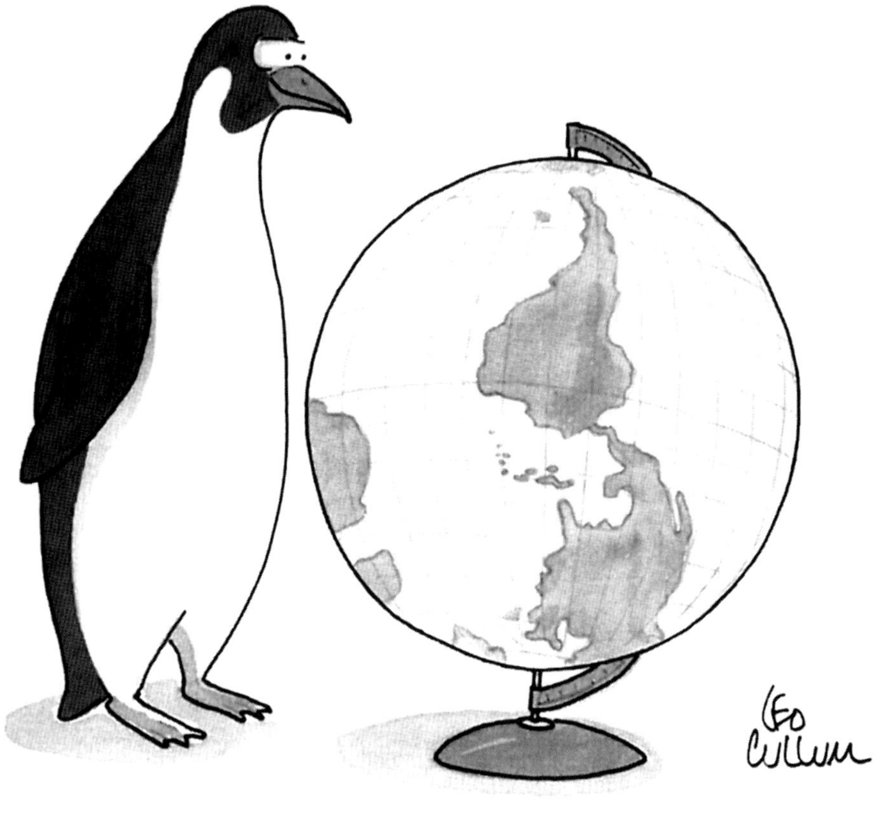
LEO CULLUM

*"So . . . can I call you?"*

"*Life is beautiful,* and *it's messy.*"

SONGBIRD

RECORD LABEL BIRD

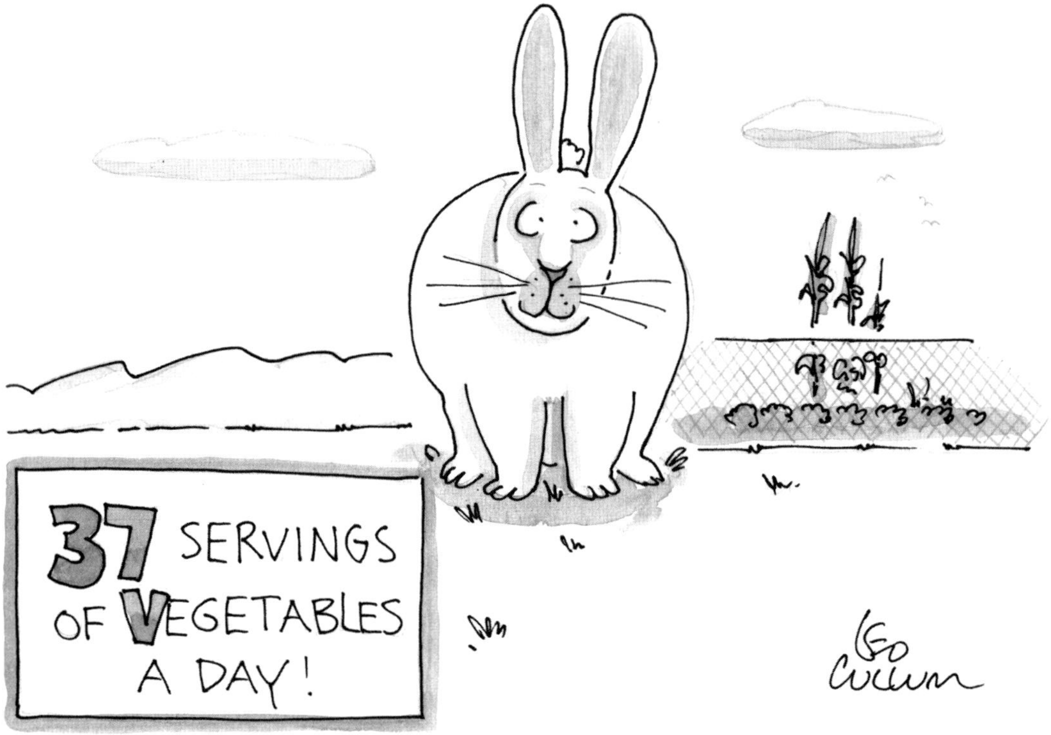
37 SERVINGS
OF VEGETABLES
A DAY!
LEO CULLUM

"I'll have whatever you recommend but smother it in cheese."

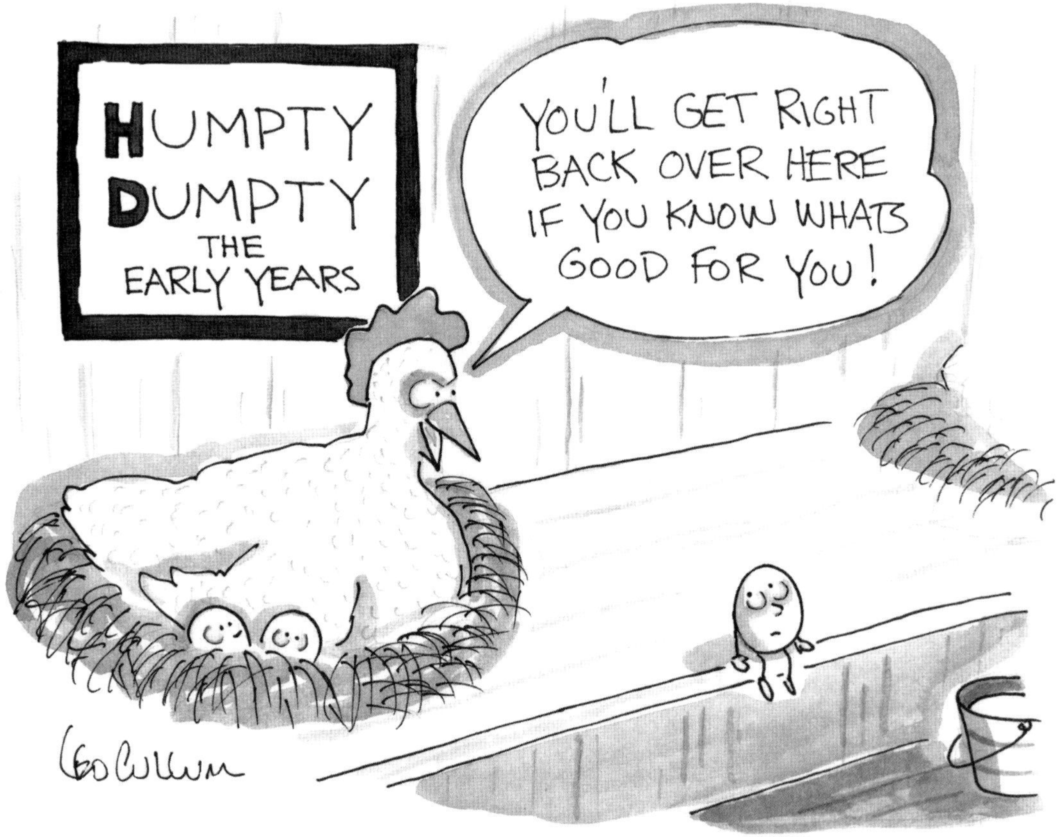
HUMPTY DUMPTY THE EARLY YEARS
YOU'LL GET RIGHT BACK OVER HERE IF YOU KNOW WHAT'S GOOD FOR YOU!
LEO CULLUM

"*I didn't go to the office today, I went to the zoo.*"

*"Please, Al. You know the backstroke scares the children."*

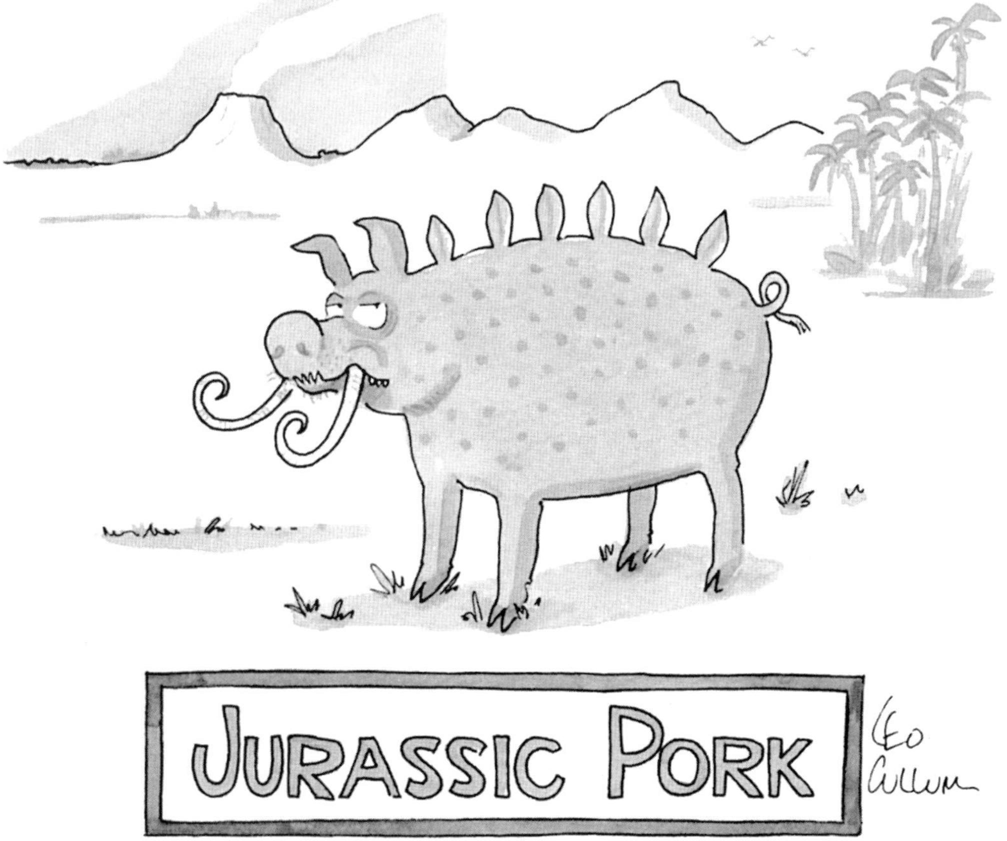
JURASSIC PORK
LEO CULLUM

"*When you first met, didn't you find it attractive that he was a free-range chicken?*"

*"Of all my husbands, I believe the first one tasted the best."*

"Current events? I can't even keep up with the current."

*"It wasn't so much losing the race, it was losing the shoe contract."*

"I'm a free woman. Edgar tried to cross the road."

*"If this deal goes through, there'll be room at the trough for all of us."*

*"Where are the car keys?"*

*"I think of myself first as an American, then as a bird, then as a Rufous-sided Towhee."*

*"I think I'm mystery meat."*

"On the other hand, if we walk upright we can carry attaché cases."

"I know I should fuggedaboutit, but I can't."